CW00969194

Making Music

Making Music

Revised

Patrick Cotter

Three Spires Press

First published by Three Spires Press in 2009
This revised edition published in 2022

Three Spires Press
11-12 St Stephen's Street,
Off Tower Street,
Cork City,
Ireland.

threespirespress@gmail.com

www.patrickcotter.ie

ISBN 978-1-873548-61-5

Cover image: *Assemblage No. 3* by Patrick Cotter

For Håken Sandell & Thomas McCarthy

Acknowledgements

Grateful acknowledgement is made to the editors of the following periodicals where a number of these poems as earlier versions have previously been published:

The Cork Literary Review, The Endicott Review, Poetry Ireland Review, The Salmon, The Shop, The Stony Thursday Book.

Some have also appeared in the following anthologies:

The Backyards of Heaven: Contemporary Poetry from Ireland and Newfoundland & Labrador; The Great Book of Ireland; The Living Landscape Anthology; Raven Introductions No. 5.

This volume constitutes a revised text of the 2009 edition.

Contents

Making Music

The opinions expressed in these poems are not necessarily those of the poet

St Barahane's Butterflies

The handcupped Red Admirals whose
escape I had aided, jerked inside again
to the high-ceilinged room, convulsed
on August nectar. One with wings
holed and threadbare. Their flickering
semaphore gibberish to our eyes. What
they sought with frequent returnings –
a mystery to all our wondering. I stood
on chairs. My kindness doubted as my fists
stealthed after them. My fingers, unfolding
and folding caged them. Their tiny faces
stayed inexpressive. No butterfly tongues
uncoiled snake-like to lick me, but
wings kissed like fluttering eyelashes.

Protecting the Eaters of Prayers

For the black cat on my windowsill is an eater of angels.
He paws at the invisible to me, high, on the outside
of the pane. For the white ruff on his neck and chest
is the colour of angel blood. For the likes of Gabriel

and Azakiel have platelets in a minority of red.
For in full health the dull grey stream in an angel's
veins turns silvery in its lungs. For purring
is a terrestrial dialect of angel speech.

And this black cat purrs like a castrato warbles.
For this vibrational lure is his deadliest decoy.
For when the marrow of angels is nowhere
in reach he practices, toys, with sparrows, pigeons,

crows. For his fur in darkness reflects the glow
of spritely eyes which only spritely eyes can see.
For in a past life Egyptians made a mummy of him
to expel the angels of Moses from their tomb.

For a cat's immunity extends to eight punishments.
Seven times already have I pushed him from a height
for consuming angels. For he lingers by my prayers
which are like, to an angel, nuts to a garden sparrow.

The Hobbyist

Not rich enough to grant himself a send-off as great
as the Emperor Chin, he opted to treat his baby finger
to a tomb, lavish, bijoux, to die for. First he dug a trench
huge at 1/72nd scale in which to inter five boxes of unbio

-degradable Airfix knights, swords and lances bristling
in ranks. In a pan in which he had once fluxed pewter
ingots for moulds of Napoleonic grenadiers he melted
commemorative sovereigns and once-upon-embargoed

Krugerrands. Springboks re-formed into bracelet-charm
bulls and warhorses: offerings for toy-town deities.
Forty-seven veterinary thermometers he snapped in two
to extract mercury enough for a miniature lake, laid-out

in a mausoleum he carved himself from smooth
Connamara marble. Mock jade idols formed from
lumps of desiccated viridian he arranged in a circle
surrounding the soapstone casket lined with butterfly

-motifed purple silk. Then he tired of Chinoiserie
and began to study coffee-table tomes on Egyptology.
He copied varicoloured silhouettes of Amun and Isis,
Horus and a chorus line of nubile kohl-eyed lasses

with Louise Brooks-style bobs onto panels of modelling
balsam, before slicing the pre-embalmed thumb of his right
hand; entombing it along with all his skill, so no finger
afterwards could receive as good a burial.

Angel Patriot

There is a black feathered angel who has skin
pale as bleached vellum. His eyes are the blue
of synthetic ice. He wanders the parquet floors
of the Crawford Art Gallery sniffing at the post

-nineteenth century exhibits: the canvasses
which proclaim "God is dead" and the conceptual
installations which disdain craft and persistence.
That first time he was astonished by my own open

-mouthed perceiving of him and immediately
raised a frosted finger to his lips so the nearby
class of long-robed Limerick convent girls
would learn nothing of him. "I have three arias

and five choral symphonies running simultaneously
through the chambers of my many cerebra," he confided,
but still had a spare string of neurones to listen
to me. All I had were the usual inquiries which

he patiently answered for the first time in decades.
His name could not be enunciated but sounded
only by running a silver comb through the final three
feathers of an angel's right wingtip. Early in the Godless

century he had been the guardian of a gifted boy
who yearned to paint but was so poor he could draw
only by scraping slate flagstones with flints of lime.
In his short life the boy haunted the gallery and expired

of consumption here one afternoon. The angel had stayed
ever since. "Are you a painter?" he said, his face filled
with concern for himself. Why after a century of anonymity
should he be open now to the probing of my eyes? When

I confessed to being a poet, and a minor one to boot,
he was appalled. "But I have no interest in poetry."
I calmed him by assuring him I had no need
of his guarding and would not make him leave

the gallery. "I'm Godless too," I told him.
The conflict of relief and disgust simultaneously
on his face was beyond the reach of any actor.
We still meet whenever I call in. Lately he was taken

by the Daniel Maclise exhibition. When I told him
Maclise was described as being of the *British* School
in the Prince of Wales Museum in Bombay
he became apoplectic. Angels are nationalist too it seems.

The Unembroidered Cloths

Only the young so sullen
need pay their way across
the Styx, slipping their shilling

to that cheerless ferryman.
His eyes barely participating
in his smile. When our window

on the world starts to blur
our skin and hair fade in lustre
it gets easier to walk on waters

of that odious river unawares
until the loveless Underworld
surrounds us like an animated

spreading cloth, dark at our feet.
And we awaken to find ourselves
treading on our own nightmares.

White Plaque Blues

The development of Alzheimer's disease is thought to be associated with the death of certain brain cells due to the build-up of an insoluble protein called amyloid-beta to form white plaques.

It begins with a word that won't come.
Later, images of a moment ago
absent as if it never happened.

As if nothing, not even time
which left a gap when it truanted
trotted off, like an over-appreciated

girl who gives no thought
to whether her ass is viewed
as she sashays away. Except her

you see going, not now, not
a moment ago, not in this
foreshortened room narrow

as an empty skull, black
as tooth cavities, wide as the pain
which fills it, swallowing it,

like the pinhole in the dyke
that sucks an entire regional sea
through to the wrong side of the wall.

What Is Not So Widely Known

Angels were not designed to be God's messengers
but are accidentally equipped to pass between
the permeable worlds of God and men.

God musters the force to compress himself
into man's form only every fifty millennia or so.
First time was as that trial piece Neanderthal

thoughtful and loving to be sure but made so
ungainly, so simply rough by all that ice, that light
so thin. How even angels, with their lesser capacity

to amuse, could be so much prettier, more delicate
occurred to God as he was gored by a woolly rhinoceros
before a scheduled ascension, and so he resolved to fashion

his next Sapiens as sculpted and as poised as a wingless angel
might be, but one still in need of the occasional instruction,
divine prodding, between major geological shifts. Prayer

works occasionally for Sapiens. But the medium of angelic
communication is all one directional and the winged precursors
of men tire of so many terrestrial expectations to intercede,

to intermediate. After all, they still search themselves
for the whereabouts of that horticultural entity
known as Eden. It stopped being a game long, long ago.

Making Music

The beautiful long-haired girl of my acquaintance
no yet-to-be lover, crying into my shoulder
convulsed with anger and remorse at the injustice of fate.
Beside us, the tall spangling tower from which

she had just travelled down, so much more slowly
than the silver flute she had dropped by accident
from altitude, the flute which, with every increase
in velocity, acquired gram upon gram of weight

until striking the anonymous innocent beneath,
bore right through his cranium, to stick in his no-longer
ageing windpipe. His last tune was a bar of Purcellian
funeral march gurgled through streamings of allegro

blood. As she whimpered I clasped, reassured
the modest tin whistle in my left-hand breast pocket.
My tin whistle, which has never risen above
the pitched roof of a three storey town house.

Lost Things

Like the doll who lost first her left
shoe, pink and plastic, then gradually
as in a preplanned list, her eyelashes
right hand, bead necklace, voice

from her internal box, all her hair
until one day in the toy chest all
that was left: one hollow unbendable leg
next to the silver Aston Martin with its

ejectable seat (bearing gun-toting Asian)
still travelling somewhere through the
universe (in a magpie's beak? buried below
ground hauled by worms?) like a long forgotten

probe, bearing an indecipherable message
from a long extinct planet for the pocket-sized,
lead-shaped Dictator (originally handpainted)
— a Victorian limited edition, craved by collectors

who monitored its descent through my family's
generations to my scion's negligent hands which
regularly now are thrust under his bed, amidst
the detritus of paper, cloth, plastic which constitute

a cloud of alternative reality in which his cellphone's
power cord may roam seeking to conjugate
with an obsolete walkman or primitive, chiming
child computer which never grew up to know the internet.

Memories and Enemies

The archived monochrome moments of our past seem more
ancient than our memories. I remember my days concurrent
with the Tet Offensive as a surfeit of colour, skies azure, green

swards, tall swaying stalks battling with the yellow of caterpillar
-infested ragwort for supremacy. Heat rising from the spotted
furnace of the ladybird's encrypted back. All these memories

so unlike the many reels of stock images we must show our
children to teach them of men's cruelty. Cold as grey and shade.
Such as a man having a gun placed to his temple, blood gushing

as from a hose, darkly like a spray of undercoat before he slumps
at the feet of his murderer. His kerbside suffering recorded
but chromatically unreal, more distant, less troublesome; mythic

like a tale of wolf 's teeth, meaningful but merely cautionary,
harmless in the now. Sometimes our children forgive the children
of our ancient enemies. How will we forgive those in high-resolution?

Thoughts of the Rich Young Aristocrat After Meeting Jesus

Resembling a shrivelled lump of camel dung from the desert.
His beard dustridden, liceridden and matted like the mane
of a toothless old lion. He descended amongst us, scattering

his jewelled-bedecked thoughts of love and forgiveness.
Never before had I seen such devotion paid by so many
to such a miserable-looking mendicant. But after I listened

to his words, his words and a voice like water falling, I too
wanted to lose myself to him, to follow him to the ends
of the dunes, to flee to his domain of happiness. But when

he answered my question with: "Not the gateway.
Not Cleopatra's needle. Not the stone taller than the tree
but the needle which drew the gold through the seams

of your satin." When he gave me that answer I could only die.
Since I know a girl of wealth with eyes of fire whose love I desire.
I think of her now in her patio of sunflowers, imagining the sapphire

-laden casket I might bring to her or the coolest purple silk
from the shoulders of an Eastern princess. With her gold and her silver
must she too tumble into fire, while the whores with whom he cavorts

can breathe forever in his company?

How to Acquire a Divine Housepet Method Three

Mumble the mumbo-jumbo — cold code
of the secretly inducted and see, out of dark
matter invisible in your own living room
angels come into being, not as juveniles

but as miniatures who still will play
with toys if you let them: Lucifer
and Michael action figures, Eden sets
with snakes, fruit trees and the spare

ribs of bulls, rams, stags, etc. Watch
them play without the absorption
or concentration of a human child
but feuguing the nonchalance,

detachment of the great self-aware
Cold Fuser, filling flesh with blood,
planets with storms, as afterthoughts,
nano-dreams, sneezes.

Saint Catherine Of Siena's Ecstatic Vision Of Her Wedding At Graball Bay, Near Crosshaven, Co. Cork

In Graball Bay that day the mist intruded
from the sea, briny, opaquing the air. A smoothened
shard of glass, worn by the rubbings of sand;

the tramplings of crustaceans; the swirling embraces
of the waves, glinted like an eye, until like a swallow
through a cloud, it vanished unexpectedly, midtidings.

With a troop of winged trombonists hovering
patiently by his side, Gabriel's feathers fluttered
and susurrated like leaves. I found myself slightly uneased.

For my matrimonial march the mist parted like a crowd.
The angel trombonists heralded my steps. The horns
of Roche's Point and the *Inisfallen* boomed heartily out

while gulls and guillemots shrieked wildly in celebration.
Not for an iota of eternity did I doubt my lover would come
wounds brandished for all to see. When he did arrive I sang my song:

My lord bridegroom's blood is honey to my kisses.
From his shredded heart is fashioned my bouquet.
His suffering expression makes me seep with pleasure.
His kindness, forgiveness enrich my soul's reflet.

King Solomon himself composed the prayers we would say:
Your love is more beautiful than wine....
Your name is an oil poured out....
Draw me in your footsteps, let us run....

I myself was so beautiful and resplendent some local girls
mistook me for the Blessed Mary. A little boy ran round
and round a rock in some mocking dance until tripping,

he split his head upon the stone, letting his blood gush
out macabrely. To seal my matrimony, delicately
My Lord Bridegroom fitted around my waiting finger

a holy band of covenant; not a band of tarnished silver
or tainted gold, but a malleable band of His Holy Flesh
sliced since infancy. The local peasantry was much impressed

A place of pilgrimage was what they made this place (a beach
where little boys peed in the sea). where the Blessed Virgin
was remembered to have worn the holy prepuce.

Saint Catherine of Siena
Saint Catherine of Graball
Saint Catherine of Siena

Saint Catherine of Crosshaven
Siena is more euphonious than Crosshaven
but Crosshaven is more sacred than Siena

Water & Air

I used to swim
I used to fall

The souls of angels will not part from their bodies
- not even under water. Otter is the form an angel
takes when it wants to swim, when air is not sensual
enough, when air fails to squeeze and to hold,
fails to stop you from falling when you turn
on your back and let go like you can in water
with the river rushing fast below you and around
you, getting between you and all the world
and everyone and everything in it. But if you
are not an angel do not repudiate air because
water will slip between even you and your soul.

On Not Being Kavanagh

I dream of composing kerbstone threnodies
and lamppost lieder. Weathered pebbledash

and cracked pavement are my demesne
and milkseeping dandelions struggling up

from dry gutterdirt to proffer nutant, droopy
flowerheads. Ants too inhabit this dusty domain

sporadically gnawing at stranded caterpillars
or huddling duncy aphids from infrequent

leaf to infrequent leaf. The honking remonstrances
of impatient automobiles vie with the dull

thrum of a factory for the neighbourhood anthem.
My reveille is the seagull's cry on its ariel lurch

to the river. Winged rescuer of discarded sewage
valiant hunter of porcine giblets spewed

from the slaughterhouse cellar, I rise to your call
ready to inspect my cemented estate, to traipse

over acrettes of tarable concrete, to examine
the productivity of windowsill boxes or the efficacy

of manhole drainage systems. Sometimes with my
neighbours I discuss the progress of the canine

distemper eradication scheme or else merely walkabout
pummelling the ground with my *Airwair* heels.

All You Need to Know About Books by Angels

Books containing the songs of angels are rare
yet anyone who wants a particular tome
eventually can track their copy down
because those interested in singing the songs
of angels are rarer still than the books they seek.
Often such books linger dust-covered, spotted
with fly-dirt in used bookstores, on shelves
down low, shelves at the back, shelves half
-forgotten behind the tottering stacks of angel
memoirs, angel novels, angel histories and angel
travelogues. Blessed are the books of angel songs.
And blessed are those who will hunt them down.

"This Is Not A Metropolitan Press Poem"

The young poet whose style and aesthetic conform
to the previous orthodoxy writes article after article
critical of the current fashionistas, their populist anthologies,
decadent enjambments; enraged that no one appreciates
his crisp, accomplished, derivative genius. Tasteful, slim
tomes of his accumulate dust in the publisher's warehouse
while review space after review space is devoted to he who
makes them all laugh or she with the long tresses and insatiable
libido. These days too will pass, he mutters as the collected
MacNeice tugs the threads holding in place his duffle coat pocket.

The young poet whose style and aesthetic
are completely original
– feels
she's
in
a
falling
lift
as yet another SAE
THUMPS heavily onto
the hallway linoleum.
The current fashionistas
have no time for what they see
as her bizarre lineation,
her tenor which they think is of a jackel or hyena.
She wonders should she stop writing all together,
if she is self-deluding
like the mediocrities
whose neat verses about ABSOLUTELY NOTHING
stain page after page
of the little magazines.
But stop she can't and on and on she scribbles,
on the backends of beermats,
the wrappings of tampons,
the moons of her fingernails.
Lipstick, ketchup,
ink, whatever comes to hand will do.
She draws the line *with* her own blood

Too Too

Everywhere he goes he's asked for evidence of his younger self
testimony of his younger self, the younger man's yearnings
turned to words. The poet must read aloud time and again
the poems he composed when young. Everywhere audiences

applaud the poems of his youth, poems by a self so distant in time
as to be another person; poems ignored in their time of composing
written by the young poet of little consequence, which now
are appreciated spilling from the mouth of the middle-aged

bard everyone pays to see, the bard who feels a charlatan,
feels a plagiarist for being so different a person from the younger
who wrote the belatedly popular verses. He alone mourns the passing
of this younger self like the passing of a lesser talented 19th century

prodigy; a quiet, unnoticed passing, none the less tragic to him
though involving no viral wave or bacillus, a passing
which took seconds or years: he doesn't quite know.
One whole weekend he sat before a mirror, slept before

the mirror wanting to witness a passing. He doesn't ever
talk about it, not even to his lover of five years who never
knew the younger self. He knows she would think it precious,
precious, too, too precious.

Now that you have turned to look at me

Take this page with you. Mark it. Or if you are
too mean or poor to buy the book, rip it out.
It has waited all this time to be yours, for you
to notice it and now you have. It doesn't care
even if you don't deserve it. A page has no control
over its destiny. So what if you don't want to frame it
after sniffing its perfume or fondling its surface?
So what if you never want to read it again?
Take it. Use it as a taper. Fold and fly it.
Twist it into the shape of a leaping flea.
Smoke it. Use it to wipe dirt from your hand
or sneeze in it. It was made to be used by you
as soon as noticed. Loved or unloved.
Unloved. Used.

No One Knows

Some say more people walk the planet's surface now
than all those buried beneath earth, those who are dust
in the air, or salt in the sea; there are more people
than bread, more people than rice, so many more

people there are not enough past lives to go around.
Before countless unnamed species went extinct
I had three undistinguished past lives, and unlike
most Chinese I have many siblings, not just now

but in the past and in new incarnations. A charlatan
in Switzerland claims one can acquire a past life
half-way through your present. You pay him a fortune
pray in a certain Orion-oriented temple and acquire

the spirit of the recently deceased. Some people are rich
and stupid enough to do this more than once. Some
have started willing their past lives to their mistresses
and grandchildren. In the rural areas of Japan

where nonagenarians are as common
as soya beans, murders have increased ninefold.
The killers are urban teens with more religion than soul.
Still, no one knows what a past life is actually for.

Stained Glass for the Blind

It is true most angels outlive their masters
like Amanakeela who loved the beauty of glass,
leaded, stained, fired. She sighed as she paused
by every varicoloured interpreter of light her master

passed by, oblivious. It never failed to fill her
with a melancholy as sweeping as an astral wind:
her master's nothing-knowing of the nuances
of cobalt, azure smalts. She laboured all his lifetime

to acquire the skill of glass which reshaped sound.
One solitary window of such musical vitreousness
she had seen, heard, smelt, in a hermitage
of haphazard rocks in a distant century on an island

the sea had long since reclaimed. Only close to her
master's death could she unveil her one worldly
creation: a glass marked with stains which revoiced
the sighing of the wind, here into the groan

of a narwhale, there into the whinny of a unicorn
and below these a pane whose stain amplified the whisper
of a breeze into the galaxy-shaking shout of God – loud enough
to stop a man's heart, long enough to launder his soul.

So So

(for D.D.)

So many geraniums in our house
so many geraniums
we are deafened by the multitude of petals
stretching open in the mornings
all at once all together
and the air is suddenly filled with perfume
as if it were swept here on the tail of a gale
so many geraniums
with a newspaper's jagged edge
I could cut the veins in my fingers
they are so soft since touching you
I listen to your voice so musical
I need never listen to another song
and your hair is enough to clothe me in the coldest storm
the paths you lead me along twist like a dancer's belly
they are so dark I need never close my eyes
so musical so dark so many geraniums
you fill my mind with so many thoughts
there are not enough windows in the world to frame them in
if you left me there's not a building high enough
that could account for my fall
so many steps would I tumble down in my own mind
so many steps so many thoughts so many geraniums.

Not Southward Enough

Right here on the edge, where the glaciers once stopped:
the Triassic fern and the island's solitary native reptile
the rarely seen, common lizard. On childhood meeting
I thought it my mind's invention or like where ghosts
vanish as soon as seen, so quickly did it dart. I had five
or six such visions over twenty summers, always
in the same place, always by surprise; no planned
safari ever made a sighting. I doubt it was the same
lizard each time, but the one family, claws clinging
to the reaching finger of Europe's last, westward rock.
As if the land itself pointed to another part, more southerly
in the tropics, where the sliver of brown quickness should go
or wait until the oven of the equator will reach up to meet it.

Journal of a Failed Angel Whisperer

(for the Acosta family)

I

I sit in the Bodega, for a moment distracted
by the bubbles in my prosecco. A bonsai-sized
angel lies asleep in my shopping bag, wings

curled in on itself, either a handsome she or
a pretty young he. It snores harp strings in no
particular tune but in a pleasant calming hum

which attracts the dusky, snub-nosed brunette
from across the vastness of table sixteen. She looks
from me to the bag and back perplexed, slightly anxious.

Her mouth opens to speak, but shuts soundlessly.
She knows me not and returns to her broadsheet's
miniscule print with lessened concentration, nostrils

flexing. I wonder what noise the angel makes
when it awakes: it's been asleep since I bought it
Along with the box of branded angel food.

2

I cradle Angel home late in the evening, way too late
for introductions. I google, but not even an elaboration
of Booleian Logic locates a care manual listed anywhere.
Where should it sleep? I can't place it in Dog's crate
or Parrot's cage. I put it on top of the wardrobe in my own
bedroom, stuffed into a cosy old slipper to sleep in.
It keeps me awake half the night with its flickering
tea-light glow so I switch it to an empty shoebox,
air-holes punched with my fine felt-tip pen.

3

At dawn Angel flips wide the box-lid and pours
out song so beautiful and strident like Vivaldi's
Gloria. The whole house awakens. Dog howls
like someone has died. Parrot mimics in the mocking
tone of a schizoid's inner voice. My mouth awakens
before the rest of me and screams *silencio!*
Angel's song drops decibels like stone
segues to the mournfulness of Durefle's *Requiem*
before Angel assumes the sullen demeanour
of an abused child. I scour Amazon again.

No manual.

4

At breakfast Dog thinks she has a new toy
until Angel tells her to sit. Cat retreats
from the kitchen all contorted backbone,
hissing and spitting. Parrot sidles up
to the newcomer with a mobster's hunch
-shouldered gait. Angel spreads its wings
sending breakfast cereal to the four corners
of the kitchen before Parrot pecks it on the arm.
Angel bows with classy servitude.

5

Angel is cavorting with the local crows.
Apparently it understands their jokes
and relates a tale of clouds and moulting
guardians. The crows fall about all black
shedding quills with slapstick abandon.
Angel gathers them up. Adds them
to the burgeoning finial of twigs
rodent skulls, red rags and motley costume
jewellery sprouting from the wardrobe's crest.

6

Cat plops a decaying blackbird at the front door.
All but rings the bell with his triumphant mewing.
Waits with the eagerness of a Fedex official
as I acknowledge delivery. Angel and Parrot
recoil at the blackbird's putrid odour,
won't let me near them until I've washed my hands.

7

The sky drops poorly pigeons
like the swooning seed of the sycamore.
Parrot and Angel watch aghast
from an upstairs window as pigeons
spread spew on the ground from both ends.
One pigeon burbling in a strange accent
is pecked to a pulp by the others.
Later in the week Parrot huddles
in his cage as Angel sniffles.
I cut Uniflu tablets into miniscule pieces.

8

I awake to Parrot plucking my eyebrows.
I'm about to rejoice at this new untrained trick
when Parrot launches into a lecture:
"You don't own us, we're not your property
blah, blah, blah, squawk, squawk, squawk,"
- a long West Coast new-think diatribe.
Dog yaps approvingly from the doorway.
"Who the fuck said you could come in," I shouted.
Dogs must know their place.
Angel tut-tutted from his finial between sneezes.

9

I opened my eyes to Angel hovering above me
more luminescent than usual. Boy was I hot
like the proverbial fires. Angel beckoned
and I radiated upwards out of the oven
of my body, glancing behind to see myself
all sweaty and pale. Angel too, slumped
colourless on the wardrobe feathers akimbo
bluebottles playing tag all over him,
so unlike his beckoning apparition shielding
my eyes now with his outspread wings
from the sight of Cat picking at my toes
Dog chomping my face off trying to waken me.
Parrot nowhere to be seen.

Las Vegas June 2006

Rumours

There was Alison O'Leary from Gregg Road
who couldn't stop chewing on her own hair
long mousy strands, so course and so abundant

no one noticed the absence of hundreds
from her scalp. Though naturally sinuous,
their own long weight pulled them straight.

They curled up in her belly like a nest
of indigestible vermicelli, blocking all passage
of food, so she died. Then there was the nameless

girl from Pearse Road joyous on her honeymoon
in Majorca, nineteen seventy-one, an early
chartered flight, who without knowing ate

an exotic roseate-tinged lettuce-head with a raw
reptilian egg hidden in its clusters of organic tulle.
In three weeks it hatched inside her a creature

replete with teeth, four feet with claws which gnawed
away at her insides as it grew from the size of a worm
so she died. A sad little girl near the Lough played

all alone at shop, with blue mussel shells for bank notes
and on her vegetable stall yew berries, stingless nettles
leaves of dock and digitalis. As her own customer

she sucked the sweet red flesh from the yew fruit
before spitting away the poisonous kernels. Of all
the leaves digitalis seemed least bitter and most crisp.

With white and lilac blossoms capping each of her digits
(except her toes) she ate wads of the greenery
until her heart stopped, or so it goes.

Angel on Holidays

Angel failed to pack his feathers on his trip
to hell, fearing the furnace heat would sweat

them out of his pores and they would curl up
like dried-out fallen leaves. He left his lyre

at home in case it would melt and as he departed,
the strings, aided by a celestial breeze, chimed

like the whines of an abandoned dog. He felt no guilt
leaving them behind. He knew it was going to be just

a short trip so he wouldn't miss these things and they
shouldn't really miss him. He brought shades for his eyes

made of slate worn so thin it became translucent
and an unction against burns made by some old Amun

Ra temple priest who had struck it lucky in the days
before Christ and Mohammad and still got to enter

heaven. But when he arrived in hell it was out of its
usual season. Even the inmates complained of the cold

— long past the stage of cool relief. His feathers, neatly
respectfully, packed in a glittering casket, the lyre

whose playing might have improved the circulation
in his pinkies: these things he now visualised on a trip

he finally realised was going to be way longer
than he could ever have known.

Angel Strangely Hidden

Not just with wings concealed passing on the street
or walking invisibly through a room when a subject
shivers. Not poised by our lips silently listening, nor
arguing with a devil on our shoulder. Not only any
of these expected things but also, not rising suddenly
wing-tip first out of our morning cereal. Not sliding
into the fricative space above your lover's skin. Not
hanging nonchalantly from the fluent shower head.
Not swirling with the laundry inside the thick-glazed
windowed, door. No, no, no. Strangely somewhere else
entirely, leaving one feather here, one little feather there
in an eider-free home.

Courthouse Steps

The stenographer has observed them for years
without ever making a record, but constantly
considers them between sustainings and
objections, laughter and contempt, pleas

and contritions. In the rain they are grey
but in the sun a polished white, worn smooth
by the condemned and their associates.
Not only murderers and thieves but innocents

and would-be divorcees tread here without
a thought for the monotone marine garden
at their feet: the courthouse steps are compressed
crinoids, millions, disarticulated fragments, waiting

for the drizzle to finally dissolve them, to wash them
into the gutter like melted petals. Fragmented humanity
ebbs here too as waves lacerated on a jagged rock.
Pigeons waddle aimlessly, crapping everywhere

while amid the blindfolded statuary of Justice
jackdaws consult, hooded like joke executioners
their shoulders stooped in judicial conspiracy
crapping more purposefully from a height.

Jaded

Glimpses of perfect teeth clad in perfect gums,
incisors, sharp as scimitars, but harmlessly
ceremonial. The jade necklace glows on your

chest with the moon's klepto brightness.
Light like a forwarded email bouncing
everywhere. The green a perfect tone

for your olive skin, singing like an Auden
libretto. At every side of me acquaintances
who greeted you. Still, they failed to see how

(no longer so much an irritation, more
a dispensation) I felt myself growing less
substantial — each passing moment you failed

to look — grey and invisible and fading by
the second. Even when your eyes turned
in my direction: gravid failure of sight.

Sludge

The semolina, the crows would not eat
perfect but for the fermenting tang of milk
too old, lying in sludge — waiting to be scraped

-up again and dropped in sticky lumps in the big
plastic wheelie bin, a fate determined days before.
A fate I tried to divert it from. How nicer to be eaten

somehow, to be someone's or something's tummyfill
rather than landfill decomposing improperly amid
the foils and cellophanes, the enduring-for-a-century

polythene? Much like I would divert my distilled
unconsumed emotions after you've gone, trawling
the pubs, confirming lack of an appetite among

the bargirls, leaving my feelings to fester slowly
amid the detritus of fragmented notions, vague
sensations, undegradable hurts.

Angels have not one heart but two

Each the size of a large man's fist.
One powers the wings alone,
thrusting blood along dedicated
arteries infused not with mere O_2 but O_4.

Nothing good comes from having two
hearts dying at different times.
Some angels die with their wing heart
working still and fly for years reflexively

in the stratosphere of their fourth dimension.
Saddest are those whose wing hearts give way
before the heart for walking and thinking.
Their last days crawl in time. They feel lessened

in dignity and their neuronal clusters charged
with analysing grief annex those which once
commanded flight, amplifying their anguish,
cancelling their capacity for noticing pain in others.

Angel Butcher

Angels are never buried. Never cremated.
They are disassembled with liturgy man
has never heard, with knives and saws
of material lost from the periodic table.
Although their blood is casked to ferment
it never tastes like wine. When the hearts
plop from their cavities, they are shredded
like a puzzled flower or exploded fruit.
Every angel of the Celestial Order of Butchers
has defletched a dead brother, thinking:
one day this will be me — yet always failing
to expect, through the ages of disintegrating
moons, how quickly that time will come.

The True Story of Aoife and Lir's Children

Fragmentary Evidence

And when they came to Lir's hill those four children were their joy and delight, for the beauty of their appearance, and it is where they used to sleep, in beds in sight of their father Lir. And he used to rise up at the break of every morning, and to lie down among his children.

— *Gods And Fighting Men* by Lady Gregory

So fond was he of them that he had them sleep in a chamber near his own, so that they should never be far from him, and in the early morning he used to rise from his bed as soon as they were awake, to talk to them, to tell them old tales and to pet and fondle them.

— *Irish Sagas and Folktales* by Eileen O'Faolain

I Aoife's Voice

I am the high-pitched whistle that worries the house
when winds are blowing. Snow-flakes show my shape
in flurries of patterned air when it is snowing. On calm

days I hide in the fissure of a rock or wrap my constrained
spirit in the high branches of a sycamore, leaves
trembling like wings restrained. My name is Aoife

whom masculine poets have much maligned
with rhyming lies, with the viciousness of rats or stoats
suppressing the truth of children's cries. What huge

misfortune ever to have met the monster Lir.
I still can recall how naif we were that first meeting
we all regret; his first wife dead, his face feaguing grief.

My foster sister Aobh was Lir's first choice, she being
youngest and more dutiful. As melodious as any harp
was her voice, her eyes were polished sloes made gleeful.

Blackberries withered on the stalk stared back at us
six months later. Her belly rounded; unable to talk
Melancholy gnawed at our cherished sister.

2 Wedding Night

How expertly in the world of men he held
in secret isolation the brutality of his heart.
Our bridal chamber, illuminated and perfumed;

a thousand dog roses, frail, shorn of briars
snuffled at my girly, unkissed feet. Our bed
was spread with swatches of red linen, silver

-stitched with Newgrange spirals of sun and moon.
But after the attendants withdrew I was grabbed
and lobbed and flopped upon. Even with the shock

a warble of affectionate protest rose from my throat
only to be blocked, stuffed and stoppered. I was impaled
like an apple being cored. My pudenda left haw-red

and nettle-scorched, my seepings moiling the spiral
stitching. He rose and withdrew to outside cheering.
A pathprint of shredded hope discarded in his wake.

3 Lir's Argument

Oh the evil of him! He said they would not have existed
had it not been for him. They were his seed, his blood.
They were like hairs dropped from his head which he
could pick up again, snap apart and discard.

4 Walk in the Woods

The ash trees were like sentient beings
beckoning me. Sycamore twigs snagged
my hair and the yews pressed their red fruit

into my mouth, the sweetness of their flesh
the bitterness of their seed, were like the barbed
syllables of a codified language of taste.

The message of their poison leaping
in spasms to my womb where Lir's
sprouting seed quenched its flourish.

5 Without Touch

How uncoy, pulling smiles of fakery;
their teeth bared in a misguise of joy,
their whole bodies rigid with the misery
of his stroking the neck and ears of each boy,
And yet unexpectedly, tenderness, in my malady,
they were attentive with restorative punch,
and warming wraps of badger hides, ready
with flaxen throws: tenderness, without touch.

6 The Abuser and the Abused

In those days, the solitary
gentleness touching me
was the graze of autumn
breezes: willingly seduced
by the stirrings of the air
I in turn seduced a rose
stroking with unfocussed
intense emotion its delicate
petals, until frenziedly, I
snatched its thorns, marring
hand and blossom at once.

7 Metamorphosis

Not transfigured to swans in an eye's blink
their skins turned first to the jadish scales of a skink.

They scrabbled frenziedly with hardening claws
and croaked the arid screeches of daws.

Their avian arteries' cold florets almost perished:
the pallid winter sunlight was with clouds enmeshed.

Their necks poured forth like pus congealed
feather-fletched as if from a mystic archer concealed.

The masked faces on the wilting stems of their necks:
candelabras raising orange the glow of beak's pecks.

Everything then was mute but for a fidgeting noise
as they fed, flicking the lake's surface, one girl, three boys.

Each one possessed a duller double in the rippling mirror.
A dark coot soon jerked against the grace of their shimmer.

8 The Lie of the Law

The grief of living through an age
when my sex was indefensible.
All slanders against me made credible.
To be like a thistle crushed beneath
my husband's foot. My life, my children
my hope, so easily stolen, like feathers
from a crippled woodsnipe. For him
to point at his grazes and say:
(his heart leaded with deceit)
"Look how she has hurt me!"
The law erected no hedgerow
of whitethorn around me
for protection, only staves
I might slip upon while fleeing.

9 At the End of the Day

To be damned to loneliness,
a spirit less substantial than air.
People around me impervious
to my thoughts and my being.
I pass through them as through
a rock or a leaf. Their fears and joys
thrilling me. But still I reside alone
in this strange tantrum zone
as if I were now just wrath incarnate.
I fear forgiving, and the freedom from anger
that comes from that. I fear my mind's peace
would bleed me away to nothingness,
to non-being. So I continue to grow in rage
and corrode the world with my spite.

The Dream of Angus

So many years
Before the soft key of her tongue
Unlocked my body.
- Gregory Orr

I

The undreamt life is not worth living.
Witness Angus, desolate and isolated,

although all loved him, a favourite son,
cherished for beauty, kindness, wit.

One glimpse of delight near stubbed
him out. He dreamt he washed slowly

carefully in a river of molten silver
then clambered out, dripping moon

-reflections. Reflected also was the moon
in a girl's eyes, in the glow on her breasts.

Her hair was so bright, it was a mystery:
was it a source of light like a flame

or a sharer of light, like gold?
Her breaking smile wiped clean

his brain; a smiling girl, so slender,
so raptured, sitting beside the shadow

of a yew. How she stared. Her eyes
had an appetite which said:

"Oh how I like what I see,
handsome man. How wonderful

your presence. How peaceful your
strength. How strong your silence."

2

When he startled awake, one small
white feather shuddered on his chest.
It was only a dream, but it recurred,
nightly, without mercy. All his waking

hours he vainly charged his wits to draft
an image of the girl as vivid as in his sleep.
He rode each day, hopelessly, in all
directions, as far as his horse could carry him,

to meet her, to touch. Soon the grief, grumbling
in the pit of himself, blent with the writhings
of hunger: honeyed oatcakes and mead-dipped
venison greened foul as his body wasted.

All he could do was lie still in bed thinking
on her and her smile, feeling the flesh drip
from his bones like pig's fat on a roasting spit.
Each morning a white feather was plucked

from his chest. He told no one of his dream.
His wasting was a mystery. Druids intoned incantations.
They fingered his body from scalp to heel, searching
for growths and the wartings of revengeful spirits.

Nothing deterred his wasting. In his dreams
he was still a strong and purposeful man, striding
out of the waters in front of her, while awake
he had not the power to roll from his own cot.

3

Ferne, the physician of Coud was called.
He with the gift of scrutinizing
a settlement's stream and deducing
how many were ailing. A mere glimpse

of a man's face revealed to him the root
of his disease. He knew men morbid
with love for their brother's wife, or even
their stepmother. He insisted on speaking

to Angus alone. "Who is this woman you love?"
Angus spilt his story like milk from a goat's teat:
the stream, the yew, the girl, the feathers.
Ferne knew, as sure as his own heart-beat,

this girl had to be. No pure dream wasted men.
I have no time to tell how Ferne found the girl,
not enough breath to tell the lengthy tales
of bloodlettings or of the trickery that stood

between Angus and the girl whose name was Cáer.
Cáer was daughter of Ethal, Ethal Anbuail.
Only after three score of his men had heads
hacked from their shoulders, only after Ailil

and Medbh of Connacht threatened to unravel
his own neck to ragged sinews, did Ethal
confess how she was not his for the giving,
how he was powerless over his own self-willed daughter.

4

She would be amenable to a man just before
altering herself to the form of a white bird.

In this form she stayed all year every second year.
Angus was told to greet her on the first day

of the following Samhain when Cáer would change.
At Loch Bel Dracon Cáer was there, looking as she did

in his dreams: a tall sinuous girl of delicate breasts
with hair of water-falling gold, and skin so pale

so like vellum, it glowed with the redness of her
own blood. When the sight of him filled her eyes

her face was as rapt as in his dreams.
"Come and sit with me Cáer." he called.

"And what is your name brazen man?"
"Angus". There was not one stirring of real distrust.

"I will only come to you if you let me return afterwards
to the water." He knew her enchantments were strong:

he could never win her by trickery or force. In truth
she was his already. As he was hers. She came to him.

For three days and three nights they lay by the lakeside
in a swan's wide nest; their wreathings, echoing the bird's

rush-work. After the third night they went to the water
and transformed to swans, spans broad as an army's flank.

Cáer clung to Angus thereafter. The rest of their lives
they spent changing from swans to gods and back.

They stayed forever enthralled and never grew
tired of the sight, or touch, or taste of each other.

How Cáer Came Into Being

This aeon of which we speak, littered newly with drumlins and moraines,
the after-gutturals of glacial dishevelment. Trees spread themselves over it
like filaments of mould over a fermenting apple: this is the godly harvest
that is Eriu. But if you are a god, sconce minutely between the leaves,
revealed there running is Oisúra, a speck upon the earth. Assured,
a rarer gift of creation is unknown for beauty, strength, speed.
Mortals and minor deities fretted for never possessing her. One such fool
was Ethal Anbúail, who ravaged the hills and all its gifts in frustrated pique.
More venison than they could eat, more antlers than they could shape,
more hides than they could wear or trade: stags by the legion were carved
by Ethal's hunt, abandoned in chunks of quivering, seeping marble to be snaffled
by ravens; gnawed by caries-ridden wolves, as common carrion. For what?
For Ethal's envy. He wanted no stag to mate with Oisúra who turned herself
to a deer for every day of every second year. Oisúra had been orphaned centuries
before, within no man's power to take or to give. Her father she had gored in revenge.
He who had begotten her. He who had defiled her. She dedicated herself to forest spirits,
swore never again, would man or beast core her. For eighty-nine years, between the quenching
of one star and the efflorescence of another, Ethal Anbúail stalked her, slitting the throat
of any stag that staggered upon Cruachàn, before starting on fawns whose balls were as green
as August chestnuts. The country was denuded of deer. Neighbouring kings raged

at this despoilment. They surrounded Ethal with swarms of spears. No stings pricked Ethal's
Dún. Winter with her acolytes, frost and snow petrified the ground, disrobed the elm
and the ash. Still the besiegers sieged. Until finally: parley. "Why do you slaughter deer?
Leaving flesh and hides to rot? Your neighbours cold, famished?" Ethal answered
with gormless honesty. As sudden as a storm, the kings' laughter shook mountain snow
as far away as Alba. "Fool! Fool! Ethal the fool!" they chanted, "Oisúra lies with nought,
not with man, not with spirit, not with plant, not with beast." They told him of Manynyn,
the druid from across the seas, intimate in ways of deer and enchantments of forest spirits.
"Summon him. Speak to him and spare our deer." The siege was lifted, the druid called.

One studied glance, was all he needed, of Oisúra's fleeting shape, to know Ethal Anbúail
would never rule this woman. "Her magic is too strong. For one hour I could suppress
its vigilance so you can lie with her as she sleeps, but this task would drain me so
I would be lame and deaf and dumb and sightless a decade afterwards."
Ethal paid the druid his own weight in silver and gold, so he would cripple both Oisúra
and himself. Subdued by a sly, impregnating narcotic lathered on a nibbled thyme blossom,
drained of her potent wakefulness, Oisúra slumbered vulnerable while Ethal slimed his way
into her, loading her with his eager stream.

After Ethal was gone, his body's heat lifted from her like a sheet.
She awoke with a drug-induced notion she was refreshed,
as if she could leap into song with happiness.
She was ignorant of the dark truth of her defilement,
until....
after a turning of the moon Oisúra was wakened by her blood's
new music rumbling through Cáer's already branching veins.
Pride at her daughter's stemming beauty, Shame and rage
at unchosen conceiving, Oisúra withered away from
the combining of it all. At Cáer's sunstruck birth,
she swore (less vainly now) as her essence
nutrified the absorbing earth:
"No man, never, without Cáer's consent".

Ethal's men stole the baby from the forest's care.
There the story paused, until another time,
upon Cáer's first bleeding, a feather entered
Angus's atrophying dream.

In 2021 Patrick Cotter published his third collection *Sonic White Poise* with the Dedalus Press, ISBN 978-1-910251-84-3.

Praise for *Sonic White Poise*

"*Sonic White Poise* Patrick Cotter's third full collection is a book of real substance by an established poet in full flow. This is an insightful, intriguing, sometimes funny report on the world. … One of the more satisfying aspects of *Sonic White Poise* is in the formal control exerted by Cotter throughout. Some of these poems, in their discursive manner, reminded me of the best of Ciaran Carson's work, the longer-than-usual lines, the thought process that is followed wherever it may go. ... The language does the work and the poems are intelligent and captivating, and deserve, require, and reward close reading."

-Richard Hayes, *Poetry Ireland Review*

"extremely impressive technique….The imaginative range in this collection is impressive….It would be difficult to find an enjambment or stanza-break out of place in *Sonic White Poise,* or to fault the perfect pacing in so many poems…..he has crafted an arresting collection with many qualities…"

-Tim Murphy, *Dublin Review of Books*

"…delightful, wry observations, all determinedly involving our every sense. Cotter is a story teller and a crafter of allegories. It's clever stuff, a joy to read aloud, rhythmic, melodious…Cotter has the knack of making you care for his eccentric characters, feel their pain and dilemmas, hope for a gentle outcome."
Melissa Todd, *Confluence.*

Patrick Cotter's *Perplexed Skin* was published by Arlen House in 2008.
ISBN 978-1903631843

Uunusual in its own way is Patrick Cotter's debut, *Perplexed Skin.* Its title sums up the book's concerns, which are chiefly with the romantic and sexual, but also with what it means to be comfortable - or not - in one's own skin. Cotter is well-known in literary circles as well as for his work with translation. All the more refreshing, then, to find a poet working within the "village" of contemporary poets but in a voice all his own; one which is unfashionable in the best sense.
Cotter clearly relishes language as much as he does sexuality: "Your mouth was a moist gourmet dessert" (Butterfly Girl); "A tigress is a girl who licks up/ all your purring like milk, before leaving you" (A Tigress Is . . .). He can be witty, too, as in 'The Singing Bichon', a nicely-judged study of dog-owning ambivalence informed by surrealism (this poodle performs arias - but only in private). Such highly-coloured imagery often resonates with European influence: the "bonsai-sized angel" on the book's first page could come straight from the Finn Ilpo Tiihonen, while 'Purchased Wisdom' is dedicated to Håken Sandell, and one can see why from the opening lines: "Your body I strewed in cleft steaks,/ your rended head lay calmed before me". Internationalism breathes vigour into this work.
-Fiona Sampson *The Irish Times*

"Cotter is an intelligent writer, not only in the sense of having a poetic intelligence that enables him to manage his lines well, but in the sense of having a rational approach. He likes ideas, fools about with them, has a personal idiom and a sophisticated sensibility. ...... Cotter's vision of the world is not simple nor does he sing of it in rapturous tones. His mirroring of complexities shows just how mature and self-assured he is."
- Maurice Harmon, *the Cork Literary Review*

"...by the time of the last, fine sequence 'The Garden', we are in the grip of something truly special."
-Ailbhe Darcy *Verbal*

"quirky, strange and thought-provoking. There are odd ideas and disturbing imagery that are both serious and humorous. These are the kind of poems that restore your faith in well crafted, serious, original poetry."
- *Books Ireland*

The best of Cotter's writing is solid poetry, intensely imagist, and speaks deeply and sincerely to real and universal human concerns. In a poem called "Such Things Do Happen," he sketches people as glimpsed on passing trains in an intense second-person narrative. As trains come and go, so the passengers live in parallel but divorced lives. At a fleeting station break, "a solitary woman / of definitive beauty" shares an intimate, sympathetic gaze with "you." Then gone, the transient trains resume their lonely courses, and the transcendence shared for a moment is lost forever. This and other gems are subtle and beautiful chamber plays, rich vignettes scattered throughout the real world, which, as he eloquently puts it, are "operas, narratives we shall never know."
- *World Literature Today*

Patrick Cotter was born in Cork City where he still lives and works. His poems have been published in journals such as *the Financial Times, The London Review of Books, Poetry* and *Poetry Review.* He is a recipient of the Keats-Shelley Prize for Poetry. His poems have been translated into over a dozen languages and he has given readings of his work across the Northern Hemisphere. He has published several chapbooks, a verse novella and three full-length collections. His work is represented in over thirty anthologies. See also www.patrickcotter.ie.

Printed in Great Britain
by Amazon